TAUNTON TO MINEHEAD

Vic Mitchell

MP Middleton Press

Front cover: Seen on 10th April 1988 is 2-8-0 class 7F no. 53808 entering Blue Anchor with the 14.05 Minehead to Williton. All aspects of the railway's restoration skills are evident, as is the sea. (T.Heavyside)

Back cover upper: The railway has been widely admired for its restoration of freight stock. Class 6400 0-6-0PT no. 6412 was recorded on 19th March 1999 at Doniford Halt. Included is the north end of the Quantock Hills. (T.Heavyside)

Back cover lower: Dunster goods yard was the setting for another fine view of assorted goods wagons. Demonstrating shunting practices on 19th March 2005 was 0-4-2T no. 1450, which was completed in 1935. It has been on the Dean Forest Railway in recent years. (T.Heavyside)

Published February 2013

ISBN 978 1 908174 39 0

© Middleton Press, 2013

Design Deborah Esher

Typesetting Barbara Mitchell

Published by
> *Middleton Press*
> *Easebourne Lane*
> *Midhurst*
> *West Sussex*
> *GU29 9AZ*
Tel: 01730 813169
Fax: 01730 812601
Email: info@middletonpress.co.uk
www.middletonpress.co.uk

Printed in the United Kingdom by Henry Ling Limited, at the Dorset Press, Dorchester, DT1 1HD

INDEX

ACKNOWLEDGEMENTS

I am very grateful for the assistance received from many of those mentioned in the credits, also to A.R.Carder, G.Croughton, N.Langridge, Mr D. and Dr S.Salter and in particular to my wife, who has meticulously typeset my scribblings for over 30 years. Included in my appreciation is S.Edge, who has kindly supplied data relating to the WSR Photographic Archive and I.Coleby, the WSR archivist, who has examined the text and helped in other ways.

I. Railway Clearing House map for 1947

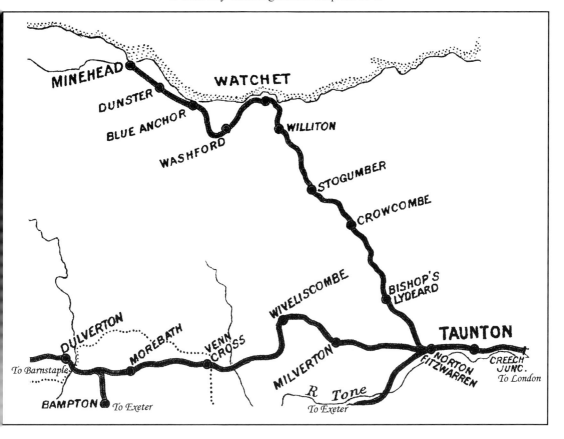

GEOGRAPHICAL SETTING

The important commercial town of Taunton is situated between the Quantock and Blackdown Hills, on the alluvium of the River Tone. At Norton Fitzwarren the branch follows a tributary of the Tone towards Bishop's Lydeard, north of which it climbs onto a much faulted area composed of Mercia mudstones, Budleigh Salterton pebbles and Otter sandstones. A continuous climb to Crowcombe takes the line to a summit, about 400 ft. above sea level, between the Brendon and Quantock Hills.

A steady descent to Williton, through the valley of the Doniford Stream, is followed by a widening of the valley as it reaches the Bristol Channel and Watchet. From here the route returns inland over the shales, marls and limestones of the Washford River valley. A summit of about 150ft. above sea level is gained at Washford, from whence the line descends onto the coastal alluvium at Blue Anchor. An almost level course, roughly parallel to the coast, is then followed to Minehead.

All maps are to the scale of 25ins to 1 mile, unless otherwise stated. They show most layouts at their maximum, although mostly in the distant past.

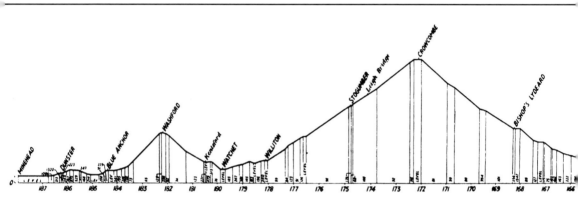

➜ II. The 1946 survey at 4 miles to 1 ins has the line from Bristol through Highbridge top right. The route to Barnstaple is on the left and the line to Exeter lower centre. The main road link between the A38 and A361 west of Taunton did not exist at that time and is shown as a lane.

HISTORICAL BACKGROUND

The enterprising Bristol & Exeter Railway spread steadily west, arriving at Taunton on 1st July 1842 and being extended through to Exeter on 1st May 1844. A branch north to Watchet was opened on 31st March 1862, although a station at the junction at Norton Fitzwarren was not provided until 1873. A branch to Barnstaple from this junction was opened on 6th August 1871. The Watchet line was built by the West Somerset Railway Co. following its Act of 17th August 1857. It was laid to the broad gauge of 7ft.0¼ins. and was operated by the B&ER.

The Minehead Railway Co. obtained an Act in 1870 to extend the branch to Minehead, the line being opened on the 16th July 1874. The train service was also provided by the B&ER.

The main lines through Taunton were fitted with a third rail in 1876, to allow for the working of standard gauge trains. The Minehead branch was converted from broad to standard gauge between 28th and 30th October 1882. The B&ER was absorbed into the Great Western Railway in 1876, but the WSR remained an independent company until 1897 and the Minehead Railway until 1922, although the GWR operated the branch.

In order to reduce congestion in the Taunton area, the GWR embarked on a scheme in 1930 to quadruple the running lines through the station and for about two miles east and west of it. Improvements to the branch followed in 1934 when two passing loops were added and the Blue Anchor - Minehead section was doubled. In 1936, the Norton Fitzwarren - Bishop's Lydeard length was also doubled.

Apart from the war years, heavy holiday traffic was handled until the mid-1960s. To reduce operating losses, diesel multiple units were introduced on 10th September 1962 and tickets were issued on the trains from 26th February 1968, although only to passengers from intermediate stations. After prolonged protestations, the branch was closed on 4th January 1971.

On 5th May 1971, a new West Somerset Railway Co. was incorporated. In 1975 it obtained a lease for the branch from the Somerset County Council who had purchased the property. A Light Railway Order had been obtained in November 1973 and services commenced between Minehead and Blue Anchor on 28th March 1976. Operation was extended to Williton on 28th August 1976, to Stogumber on 7th May 1978 and to Bishop's Lydeard on 9th June 1979. Sadly for all concerned, a number of obstacles were raised to prevent operation to Taunton again.

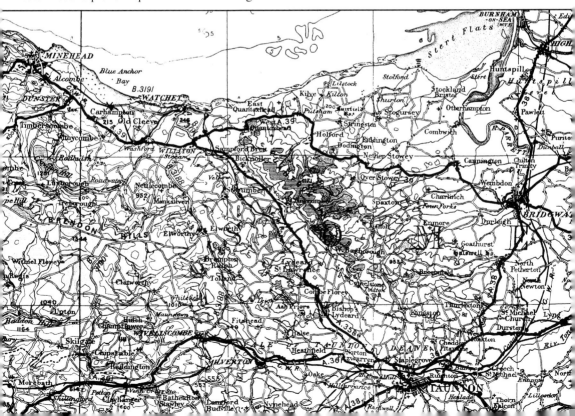

PASSENGER SERVICES

In the last years of BR operation, ten weekday services were normally provided, with five or six on summer Sundays. There were still some through trains; for example, on summer Saturdays in 1968, there were two to Paddington and two to Bristol.

The early years of WSR running are shown in the following timetables. In the Summer of 2007, there was a through train to Bristol and back on three days a week, but it was unprofitable and was not repeated.

May 1970

Taunton to Minehead — Mondays to Fridays, also Saturdays from 3 October

Miles	Station										FSO	B FSX
0	TAUNTON d	06 35	07 29	09 15	11 15	13 15	14 45	16 42	17 48	20 16	21 10	21 10
5	BISHOP'S LYDEARD d	06 43	07 38	09 23	11 24	13 23	14 53	16 50	17 56	20 24	21 18	21 25
9	CROWCOMBE d	06 51	07 46	09 31	11 32	13 31	15 01	16 58	18 04	20 32	21 26	21 45
11½	STOGUMBER d	06 59	07 52	09 37	11 38	13 37	15 07	17 04	18 10	20 38	21 32	
15	WILLITON d	07 05	08 01	09 46	11 45	13 44	15 16	17 13	18 17	20 45	21 41	22 01
16½	WATCHET d	07 09	08 05	09 50	11 49	13 48	15 20	17 17	18 21	20 49	21 45	22 10
19	WASHFORD d	07 15	08 11	09 56	11 55	13 54	15 26	17 23	18 27	20 55	21 51	22 19
21½	BLUE ANCHOR d	07 20	08 16	10 01	12 00	13 59	15 31	17 28	18 32	21 00	21 56	
23	DUNSTER d	07 24	08 20	10 05	12 04	14 03	15 35	17 32	18 36	21 04	22 00	
24½	MINEHEAD a	07 29	08 25	10 10	12 09	14 08	15 40	17 37	18 41	21 09	22 05	22b42

Saturdays — Until 26 September

Station				K		C							
TAUNTON d	06 15	07 20	08 30	09 20	10 24	11 13	12 52	14 05	15 15	17 00	17 54	19 10	21 10
BISHOP'S LYDEARD d	06 23	07 28		09 28		11 21	13 00	14 13	15 23	17 08	18 02	19 18	21 18
CROWCOMBE d	06 31	07 36		09 36		11 29	13 08	14 21	15 31	17 16	18 10	19 26	21 26
STOGUMBER d	06 39	07 42		09 42		11 35	13 16	14 27	15 37	17 22	18 16	19 32	21 32
WILLITON d	06 46	07 51	08 56	09 51	10 51	11 46	13 27	14 36	15 46	17 31	18 26	19 41	21 41
WATCHET d	06 50	07 55	09 00	09 55	10 55	11 51	13 31	14 40	15 50	17 35	18 30	19 45	21 45
WASHFORD d	06 56	08 01	09 06	10 01	11 01	11 57	13 37	14 46	15 56	17 41	18 36	19 51	21 51
BLUE ANCHOR d	07 01	08 06	09 11	10 06	11 06	12 06	13 42	14 51	16 01	17 46	18 41	19 56	21 56
DUNSTER d	07 05	08 10	09 15	10 11	11 10	12 07	13 46	14 55	16 05	17 50	18 45	20 00	22 00
MINEHEAD a	07 10	08 15	09 20	10 15	11 15	12 12	13 51	15 00	16 10	17 55	18 50	20 05	22 05

Sundays — 14 June to 6 September | Sundays — Until 7 June and from 13 September

Station	D				B			B	B	B	B
TAUNTON d	09 00	11 43	14 10	16 35	19 15	21 10		14 55	16 50	18 50	21 10
BISHOP'S LYDEARD d	09 08	11 51	14 18	16 43	19 23	21 25		15 10	17 05	19 05	21 25
CROWCOMBE d	09 16	11 59	14 26	16 51	19 31	21 45		15 30	17 25	19 25	21 45
STOGUMBER d	09 22		14 32	16 57	19 37						
WILLITON d	09 29	12 12	14 39	17 04	19 44	22 01		15 46	17 41	19 41	22 01
WATCHET d	09 33	12 16	14 43	17 08	19 48	22 10		15 55	17 50	19 50	22 10
WASHFORD d	09 39	12 22	14 49	17 14	19 54	22 19		16 04	17 59	19 59	22 19
BLUE ANCHOR d	09 44		14 54	17 19	19 59						
DUNSTER d	09 48	12 31	14 58	17 23	20 03						
MINEHEAD a	09 53	12 36	15 03	17 28	20 08	22b42		16b27	18b22	20b22	22b42

C On certain dates is a through service from London Paddington (See Table 1)

D From Bristol T.M.

K On certain dates is a through service from Oxford (See Table 1)

B (Western National) from Taunton Rail Station Bridge to Minehead Bus Station. Calls at Bishop's Lydeard (Police Station), Crowcombe (Carew Arms), Williton (Egremont Hotel), Watchet (Rail Station) and Washford (Sheppards Corner)

b Minehead Bus Station

Minehead, Watchet, Williton and Stogumber — West Somerset Railway

Miles			Mondays to Saturdays Until 30 September													Sundays Until 1 October			
				● A TThO	● B SX	C SO	A TThO	B SX		● D TThO	● B SX	● B SX		G TThO		● E	●	●	
0	**Minehead**	d	09 00	10 35	10 35	10 35	11 25	11 25	12 30	14 35	14 35	15 40	16 30	18 35	..	10 35	14 15	16 15	..
1¾	Dunster	d	09 05	10 41	10 41	10 40	11 30	11 30	12 35	14 41	14 41	15 46	16 35	18 40	..	10 41	14 21	16 21	..
3½	Blue Anchor	d	09 12	10a48	10a48	10 47	11 37	11 37	12 42	14a48	14a48	15a53	16 42	18 47	..	10 50	14 30	16 30	..
5¼	Washford	d	09 19	..	..	10 54	11 44	11 44	12 49	..	..	..	16 49	18 54	..	10 59	14 39	16 39	..
8	Watchet	d	09 26	..	..	11a01	11a51	11a51	12 56	..	..	..	16 56	19a01	..	11 08	14 48	16 48	..
9¾	Williton	a	09 31	..	..	..	..	..	13 01	..	..	..	17 01	..	..	11 15	14 55	16 55	..
		d	09†32	..	..	..	..	..	13†02	..	..	..	17†02	..	..	..	..	..	..
13	**Stogumber†**	a	09†42	..	..	..	..	..	13†12	..	..	..	17†12	..	..	..	..	..	..

Miles				● A TThO	● B SX	C SO	A TThO	B SX		● D TThO	● B SX	● B SX		G		● E	●	●	
0	**Stogumber†**	d	09†45	..	..	..	..	..	13†45	..	..	..	17†15	..	..	..	..	..	..
3¼	Williton	a	09†55	..	..	..	..	..	13†55	..	..	..	17†25	..	..	..	..	..	..
		d	09 55	..	..	..	..	..	13 55	..	..	..	17 25	..	..	11 35	15 15	17 15	..
5	Watchet	d	10 00	..	..	11 05	11 57	11 57	14 00	..	..	..	17 30	19 05	..	11 42	15 22	17 22	..
7¾	Washford	d	10 08	..	..	11 12	12 04	12 04	14 08	..	..	..	17 38	19 12	..	11 51	15 31	17 31	..
9½	Blue Anchor	d	10 15	11 05	11 05	11 19	12 11	12 11	14 15	15 05	15 05	16 10	17 45	19 19	..	12 00	15 40	17 40	..
11¼	Dunster	d	10 21	11 13	11 13	11 25	12 17	12 17	14 21	15 13	15 13	16 18	17 51	19 25	..	12 08	15 48	17 48	..
13	**Minehead**	a	10 27	11 19	11 19	11 30	12 23	12 23	14 27	15 19	15 19	16 24	17 57	19 31	..	12 14	15 54	17 54	..

This service is operated exclusively by the West Somerset Railway Company Ltd. to whom all enquiries and communications should be addressed at The Railway Station, Minehead, Somerset, Tel. 4996

- ● Steam train
- A 9 May to 1 June
- B 5 June to 8 September
- C 17 June to 2 September
- D 9 May to 1 June and 12 to 28 September
- E 25 June to 3 September
- G 6 June to 28 September
- † Service to Stogumber operates Tuesdays, Fridays and Saturdays from a date to be announced locally

May 1978

May 1979

Minehead, Williton, Bishops Lydeard and Taunton — West Somerset Railway

This service is operated exclusively by the West Somerset Railway Company Ltd. to whom all enquiries and communications should be addressed at The Railway Station, Minehead, Somerset, Tel. 4996

Miles			Mondays to Fridays Until 11 October								Saturdays 19, 26 May and 2 June			Saturdays 9 June to 13 September					Sundays Until 14 October					
				● A	A		● A	● B		C									● D	● D	●	● D	●	● D
0	**Minehead**	d	09 00	10 35	11 25	12 30	14 35	15 40	16 30	18 05	09 00	12 30	16 30	09 15	10 35	12 30	15 10	16 30	10 35	..	14 15	..	16 15	..
1¾	Dunster	d	09 05	10 41	11 30	12 35	14 41	15 46	16 35	18 10	09 05	12 35	16 35	09 20	10 40	12 35	15 15	16 35	10 41		14 21		16 21	..
3½	Blue Anchor	d	09 12	10a48	11 37	12 42	14a48	15a53	16 42	18a16	09 12	12 42	16 42	09 27	10 47	12 42	15 22	16 42	10 50	..	14 30	..	16 30	..
5¾	Washford	d	09 19	..	11 44	12 49	..	..	16 49	..	09 19	12 49	16 49	09 34	10 54	12 49	15 29	16 49	11 00	..	14 40	..	16 40	..
8	Watchet	d	09 26	..	11a51	12 56	..	..	16 56	..	09 26	12 56	16 56	09 41	11 02	12 56	15 36	16 56	11 08	..	14 48	..	16 48	..
9¾	Williton	a	09 31	..	..	13 01	..	..	17 01	..	09 31	13 01	17 01	09 46	11 07	13 01	15 41	17 01	11 16	..	14 56	..	16 56	..
		d	09†32	..	..	13†02	..	..	17†02	..	09 32	13 02	17 02	09 54	11 07	..	15 41	..	..	11 25	..	15 05	..	17 05
13	Stogumber	d	09†42	..	..	13†12	..	..	17†12	..	09a42	13a12	17a12	10 04	11 17	..	15 51	..	..	11b39	..	15b19	..	17b19
15¾	Crowcombe	d	..	..	..	..	..	..	..	..	..	..	..	10 11	11 24	..	15 58	..	..	11 46	..	15 26	..	17 26
19¾	Bishops Lydeard	a	..	..	..	..	..	..	..	..	..	..	..	10 21	11 34	..	16 08	..	..	11 56	..	15 36	..	17 36
		d	..	..	..	..	..	..	..	..	..	..	..	*10§25*	*11§40*	..	*16§35*	..	..	..	..	..	..	..
24¾	**Taunton (Rly Stn)**	a	..	..	..	..	..	..	..	..	..	..	..	*10§45*	*12§00*	..	*16§55*	..	..	..	..	..	..	..

Miles				● A	A		● A	● B		C									● D	● D	● D	●	● D	●
0	**Taunton (Rly Stn)**	d	..	..	..	..	..	..	..	..	..	..	..	..	*10§00*	..	*14§50*	*16§10*	..	..	..	..	..	..
5	Bishops Lydeard	a	..	..	..	..	..	..	..	..	..	..	..	..	*10§20*	..	*15§10*	*16§30*	..	..	..	..	..	..
		d	..	..	..	..	..	..	..	..	..	..	..	..	10 38	..	15 13	16 48	10 40	..	14 20	..	16 20	..
9	Crowcombe	d	..	..	..	..	..	..	..	..	..	..	..	..	10 48	..	15 23	16 58	10 55	..	14 35	..	16 35	..
11¾	Stogumber	d	09†45	..	..	13†45	..	..	17†15	..	09 45	13 45	17 15	..	10 55	..	15 30	17 05	11 03	..	14 43	..	16 43	..
15	Williton	a	09†55	..	..	13†55	..	..	17†25	..	09 55	13 55	17 25	..	11 05	..	15 40	17 15	11 15	..	14 55	..	16 55	..
		d	09 55	..	..	13 55	..	..	17 25	..	09 55	13 55	17 25	09 55	11 05	13 55	15 40	17 25	..	11 30	..	15 10	..	17 10
16¾	Watchet	d	10 00	..	11 55	14 00	..	..	17 30	..	10 00	14 00	17 30	10 00	11 10	14 00	15 45	17 30	..	11 38	..	15 18	..	17 18
19	Washford	d	10 08	..	12 02	14 08	..	..	17 38	..	10 08	14 08	17 38	10 08	11 18	14 08	15 53	17 38	..	11 48	..	15 28	..	17 28
21¼	Blue Anchor	d	10 15	11 05	12 09	14 15	15 05	16 10	17 45	18 20	10 15	14 15	17 45	10 15	11 25	14 15	16 00	17 45	..	11 55	..	15 35	..	17 35
23	Dunster	d	10 21	11 13	12 15	14 21	15 13	16 18	17 51	18 26	10 21	14 21	17 51	10 21	11 31	14 21	16 06	17 51	..	12 03	..	15 43	..	17 43
24¾	**Minehead**	a	10 27	11 19	12 21	14 27	15 19	16 24	17 57	18 32	10 27	14 27	17 57	10 27	11 37	14 27	16 12	17 57	..	12 09	..	15 49	..	17 49

For general notes see pages 2-4

The Company reserves the right to amend or cancel the timetable without notice

Note: Services between Stogumber and Taunton are subject to approval

- A Tuesdays and Thursdays until 24 May and from 18 Sept., Mondays to Fridays 29 May to 14 September
- B 29 May to 14 September
- C 9 July to 7 September
- D 10 June to 16 September
- b Arr. 4 minutes earlier
- † Tuesdays and Fridays
- § Special 'bus service available for rail passengers only
- ● Steam train

For service after 15 October see October Supplement or West Somerset Railway timetable

A 1977 timetable can be found under caption 112.

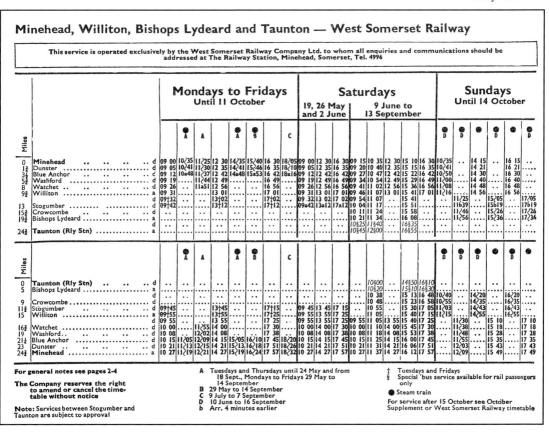

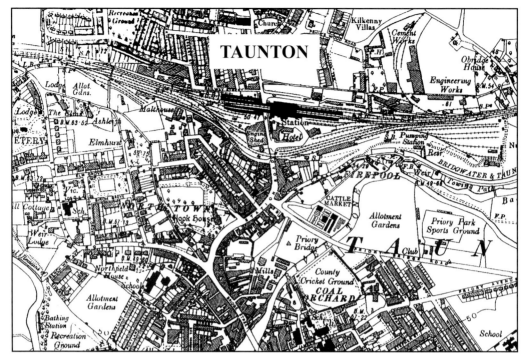

III.   The 1930 edition at 6ins to 1 mile shows two tracks bypassing the station. These were used for goods traffic and lasted until 1986. The main lines were quadrupled by 1931 and nine platforms were available thereafter.

1.   This is the London end of the station in the early 1960s and East Yard is in the distance. Its tracks were lifted in 1994. On the right is East Junction Box, which was closed on 23rd March 1987. (Lens of Sutton coll.)

2.   Leaving the other end of the station in the same era is 4-6-0 no. 7029 *Clun Castle*, which was saved for posterity. Behind it is West Station Box, which was less fortunate and was taken out of use on 12th May 1986. (D.Lawrence/H.Davies coll.)

3.   The middle of this westbound train of oil tankers on 11th October 1971 is level with West Station Box. The locomotive is no. D1039 *Western King*. (T.Heavyside)

4.　　We move on to 1st February 1978 and witness no. 31258 passing through with a down ballast train. The white clad building on the right edge had been the locomotive repair shed in the steam days. (T.Heavyside)

Extract from Bradshaw's Guide for 1866.
(Reprinted by Middleton Press 2011)

TAUNTON.

A telegraph station.

HOTELS.—Castle ; London Inn.

MARKET DAYS.—Wednesday and Saturday.

FAIRS.—June 17th and July 7th.

The town, as seen from the station, has a most pleasing appearance. It is situated in the central part of the luxuriant and beautiful vale of Taunton Dean.

TAUNTON is an ancient borough town, population 14,667 (two members), in a rich and beautiful part of Somersetshire, on the Bristol and Exeter railway, 163 miles from London. The wide and cultivated dean, or shallow strath, in which it stands is watered by the Tone (wherefore the Saxons called it *Tantun*), and overlooked by the tower of its Gothic church, which is of Henry Seventh's age. The tower is 153 feet high, of light and elegant proportions, covered over with heads of lions, &c., and set off with pinnacles, battlements and niches, in the elaborate style of that day, of which, indeed, Somersetshire furnishes many excellent specimens.

5.   Photographs 3 to 5 were taken from the footbridge shown on the left of map III. This westward view is from 12th May 1979 and has the bridge carrying Staplegrove Road in the background. No. 45041 is hauling ballast on the goods lines and passes the obsolete water tank, near the two former carriage sidings. (T.Heavyside)

Other views of this station can be found in
Westbury to Taunton, Branch Line to Minehead,
Branch Lines around Chard and Yeovil, Taunton to Barnstaple,
Bristol to Taunton, Taunton to Exeter,
plus Station Road in *Exeter & Taunton Tramways.*

6.   No. 46009 is westbound on 16th May 1979 with empty china clay wagons. In the other direction, such loads were covered with tarpaulin sheets. (T.Heavyside)

7. Trees grow on the island platform, which had been unused since 6th March 1967. The original building can be seen on the right as no. 50036 *Victorious* works the 12.10 Paddington to Penzance on 2nd September 1989. The gigantic logos did not last long. (T.Heavyside)

8. The old Repair Shop was no longer white when photographed on 22nd April 2000. The bay platform was numbered 1 from 1st May 2000, when it was available for use again. (V.Mitchell)

9. Seen on the same day, work was starting on the restoration of the island platform. The roof is on the north entrance. (V.Mitchell)

10.　The island platform was reopened on 28th May 2000 and is seen from a down train two months later, when numbered 3 and 4. The shelter is conventional, but the second poster is not. (V.Mitchell)

11.　Known as Fairwater Bridge, the bowstring girders were erected over the widened tracks, which came into use in February 1932. West Junction Box had been near its north end until December 1970. In the background in April 2000 are the sidings of Fairwater Yard. Its seven tracks formed the High Output Ballast Cleaning Yard in 2010. The route on the left was made a bidirectional relief line. In the far distance was Silk Mill Crossing, but a bridge was built in 2005-06 to replace it and this carried the A3605 over the three tracks. (V.Mitchell)

EAST OF NORTON FITZWARREN

12.   The gates of Silk Mill Crossing were replaced by these full lifting barriers on 28th October 1962 and they are seen near the end of their life. There had been four tracks here for many years. (J.Tooke)

WEST SOMERSET
RAILWAY ASSOCIATION

GALA DAY

Sunday, 7th MAY, 1978

DAY TICKET £2.00
(including unlimited travel on W.S.R. trains available)

Issued subject to
the Company's conditions   № 316

13.   No. 6233 *Duchess of Sutherland* has just left Fairwater Yard on 1st June 2008 and is bound for Bishop's Lydeard. The signal box had been on the left, but it was closed on 23rd March 1987. There were sidings behind the camera to a sugar factory in the 1930s, but they served a military depot from 1940 until 1976. (L.Robbins)

14.   The bridge frames are seen in this westward view from 16th June 2005. The structure was built to the west of the crossing. (Janet Day)

15.   The Cheshire Rail Tour ran from Manchester on 4th August 2001 and is about to pass over the up main line to reach the WSR, using the siding of Taunton Cider. They owned this part of the branch from 1st March 1983 and several specials have used it in most years, since 1990. (V.Mitchell)

16.   A few minutes later and no. 47727 had to force back a tree. The first excursion over the connection had been from Manchester on 16th June 1990, but they were very infrequent initially. (V.Mitchell)

NORTON FITZWARREN

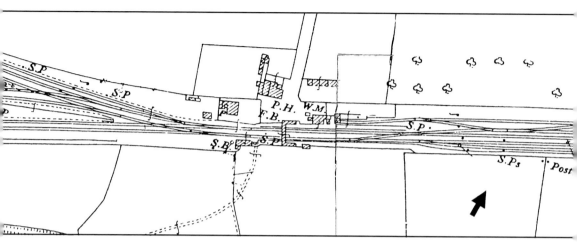

IV.   The 1929 map has the main line double track through the station and on the right they are flanked by goods lines. Upper right are sidings, which extend from the goods yard. The top line on the left is a siding; the two below it soon converge to form the Minehead branch. The route was double to Bishop's Lydeard from 8th June 1936 until 11th May 1969. The two below form the route to Barnstaple and soon converge. The lower pair represent the Exeter main line.

17.   Quadruple track reached here on 14th February 1932, when the new platforms and signal box opened. Passenger service ceased here on 30th October 1961 and freight followed on 6th July 1964. The box was on the south side of the station and closed on 1st March 1970. It had a remarkable 131 levers. (Lens of Sutton coll.)

18.   No. 50023 *Howe* is working the 13.20 Liverpool to Plymouth service on 12th September 1981. The public footbridge is also visible in the previous photograph. Up Minehead trains had used the line on the left in BR days. (J.A.M.Vaughan)

19.   We see the east side of the footbridge from a train bound for Exeter on 22nd April 2000. The two spans on the right pass over the yard of the Taunton Cider works. It ceased to use rail transport in 1992 and was demolished in 2006. The occasional Minehead special uses the line between the two fences. (V.Mitchell)

V.   The WSRA completed a turning triangle in 2012. Its southern side was formed by relaying the first part of the line to Barnstaple. East Chord allows engines to be turned without entry onto NR property. (S.Edge)

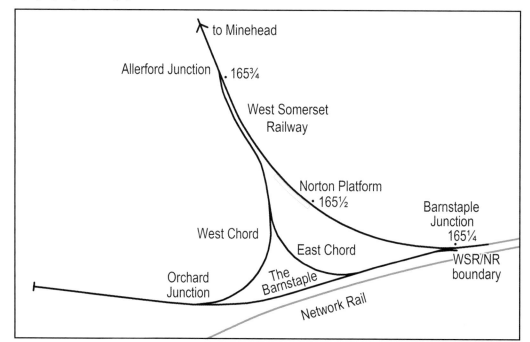

20.   The triangle is seen from about 500ft on 25th March 2011, with the main line close to the propeller. Little track had been laid at this stage, but the new platform is evident, top right. (A.Dorrington)

21.   The platform was built on the south side of the Minehead line and is seen from the cab of no. 66610 on 26th February 2011. In the background are spent ballast heaps. The platform can take four coaches and allows visitors to reach events being held on the triangle site. (L.Renwick)

22.   No. 66607 has brought ballast from Fairwater Yard on 29th October 2010. This is Network Rail's high output ballast cleaner train providing recycled material. On the main line, the train lifts dirty ballast and puts down clean as it goes. (N.Mann)

23.   The completed platform was recorded from the cab of no. 66610 in April 2010. A track on the other side of the platform was planned. The outer triangle was completed on 29th April 2011. (L.Renwick)

24.   The first steam locomotive to turn on the triangle was 4-6-2 no. 70000 *Britannia*, on 31st March 2012. It is approaching Barnstaple Junction and in the distance is the bridge seen in pictures 17-19. (M.Anderson)

25.   A short time later, *Britannia* was recorded on the West Chord as a Cross Country express races by. This was WSR enterprise at its best. The first diesel to turn was on the previous day, when a class 66 ran round a train of rail. (M.Southwood)

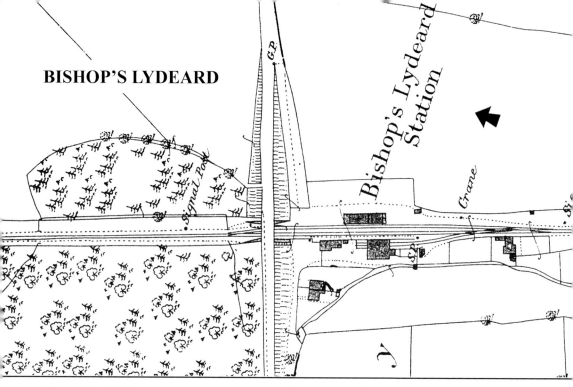

BISHOP'S LYDEARD

VI.   The 1886 survey shows a very narrow lane to the down platform and a large building on the up side. The loop was lengthened later and two sidings were added on the east side. One came in about 1906 and another served a food store in 1943-65. The new WSR has not used the apostrophe.

26.   A panorama from 8th June 1963 reveals all structures to be in good order, with the residence for the station master in the background. The station and signal box ceased to be staffed on 1st March 1970. (C.G.Maggs)

27.   Built by Bagnall in 1951 for use at Margam Steelworks, 0-6-0ST *Victor* was photographed upon arrival on 15th March 1981. Tankers would not normally be near a goods shed, but the vehicle's fine restoration could be admired in this position. (T.Heavyside)

28.   Ex-GWR 2-6-2T no. 5572 was recorded blowing off on 13th September 1987 and about to depart with assorted rolling stock. This was still in short supply at that time, hence the inappropriate inclusion of a DMU car. At least visitors could enjoy the view from its end windows. (T.Heavyside)

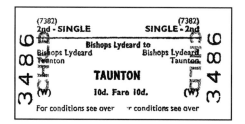

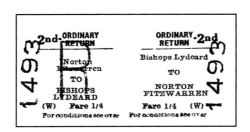

29.   Immaculate on 7th April 1991 is ex-GWR 0-6-0 no. 3205 as it simmers ahead of coaches in GWR livery. Behind the train is a long carriage siding. The wartime emergency food store is in the background. The signal box has 33 levers. (T.Heavyside)

30.   Mud abounds as 0-6-0ST *Victor* leaves with the "Quantock Pullman" on 15th March 1981. A train of this length was ideal for this small locomotive. A trolley has been placed in the traditional position, as seen in picture no. 26. (T.Heavyside)

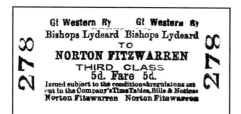

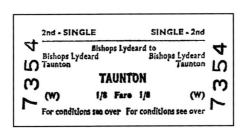

2nd · SINGLE	SINGLE · 2nd

Bishops Lydeard to

Bishops Lydeard to Taunton · Bishops Lydeard Taunton

TAUNTON

(W)   1/8 Fare 1/8   (W)

For conditions see over   For conditions see over

4 5 3 7 3 5 4

31.   Limited weather protection has always been a feature here, which was never intended as a terminus. Ex-GWR 2-6-2T no. 4561 arrives on 31st October 1991 and we gain a glimpse of the steps from the road. They were of value for those needing to use the ticket office on the left. (T.Heavyside)

32.   A temporary ticket office was erected by the up platform and is seen here on 28th April 2009. This was later replaced by a new ticket office built by the WSRA on the platform itself. New weather protection was added to the up platform, near the signal box. (L&K Daems)

33.   Nearest on 28th December 2011 is ex-GWR 2-8-0 no. 3850 and on the left is ex-Somerset & Dorset Joint Railway 2-8-0 no. 88. The buildings to the left of its train were erected by the West Somerset Railway Association in 1991-92 and contain an imaginative visitor centre, a splendid shop and a more convenient booking office. (T.Cowen)

34.   We are at the south end of the station on 13th August 2012 as Amey tamper no. DR73920 returns from work on the new turning triangle. The coaches are in a short berthing siding, to the left of which are two locomotive sidings, with pits. The line on the left in the distance forms two long carriage sidings. (R.Osborne)

WEST SOMERSET RAILWAY
EASTER FAIR 1983
DAY ROVERTICKET
Valid on

for unlimited travel on WSR trains
and admission to Fairground and Stands
ADULT £5·00

Issued subject to Company's conditions
Not transferable   № 000105

CROWCOMBE HEATHFIELD

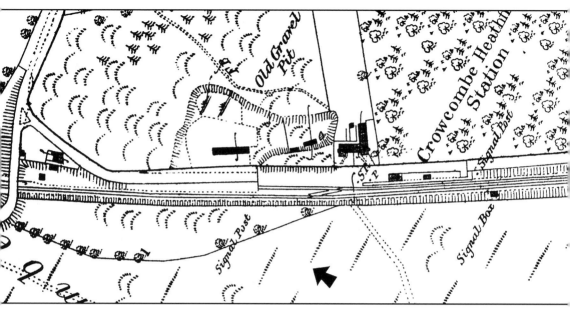

VII.   The 1889 survey indicates the isolated location of the station, a situation which still applies.

35.   In BR livery, 2-8-0 no. 53808 arrives from Minehead on 11th September 1987. The line on the left is a siding; it was extended to form a loop in 1992, which it had been until 5th March 1967, when the signal box closed. (T.Heavyside)

36. This is the south end of the station on 30th October 1988, as the same engine works the 10.15 Minehead to Bishop's Lydeard. Staff and volunteers work to control the natural invasion of the route. (T.Heavyside)

VIII. The 1946 map at 2ins to 1 mile reveals the remoteness of the station from the village.

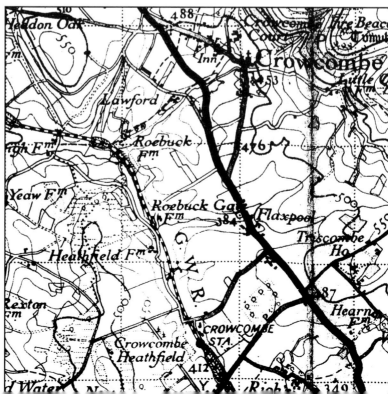

37.   The rural location is emphasised again as 4-4-0 no. 3440 *City of Truro* heads north with the 15.55 Bishop's Lydeard to Minehead on 19th July 1992. This engine became the first steam locomotive to break the 100 mph barrier, while running on the main line from Exeter in 1904. (T.Heavyside)

38.   A closer view that day shows *City of Truro* about to depart north. After decades in a museum in York, it was restored to running order and its first public appearance was on the 1958 AGM special for the Festiniog Railway Society, your scribe being one of its organisers. (T.Heavyside)

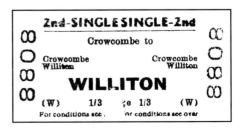

39.   GWR 4-6-0 no. 6024 *King Edward I* and GWR 0-4-2T no. 1450, with autocoach no. 178, wait on 31st March 2012 at the special event celebrating the 150th anniversary of the opening of the original WSR. This view is from the signal box, which had been brought from Ebbw Vale Tin Plate Works; the frame came from Frome North and has 29-levers. (M.Southwood)

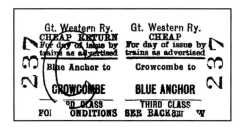

WEST SOMERSET RAILWAY		WEST SOMERSET RAILWAY
0402 FIRST CLASS SUPPLEMENT SINGLE Not valid without valid 2nd class single ticket Issued subject to Comp 's onditions 0402		1279 DOG TICKET Issued subject to Company's Conditions 1279

40.   The anniversary events continued the next day and many staff members were attired in dress of the period. Oil lamps were already standard, but no longer could you spend a penny of the Victorian type. (M.Southwood)

STOGUMBER

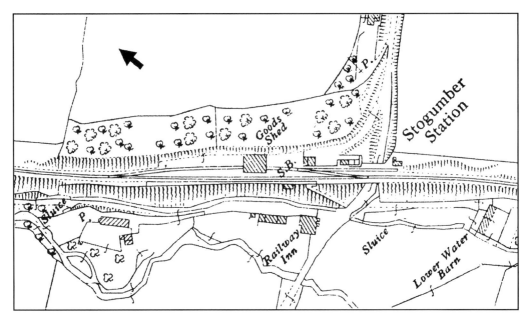

IX.   The 1904 edition has the river well below the level of the railway. As a consequence, the platform was built on the embankment and wood was used to minimise the weight.

41.   The station building was remote from the platform for the reason given. It is on the right and at the top of a lane up from the road, which passes under the line. The DMU is seen on 10th April 1988. Such units were often used in the first decade of preservation, but they did not draw the crowds. (T.Heavyside)

42. Later the same day, 2-8-0 no. 53808 appeared. The platform had originally extended to the foot crossing from the booking office. Its removal meant that the shelter was too high to use. The goods shed had been to the right of the locomotive, but it had been demolished in 1965. (T.Heavyside)

43. The James Willis Memorial Garden was in fine condition on 31st March 2012, during the special event celebrating the 150th anniversary of the opening of the line. (C.Osment)

WILLITON

X.   The 1904 edition shows that the road had been diverted over a bridge to minimise the use of the level crossing at the end of the platforms.

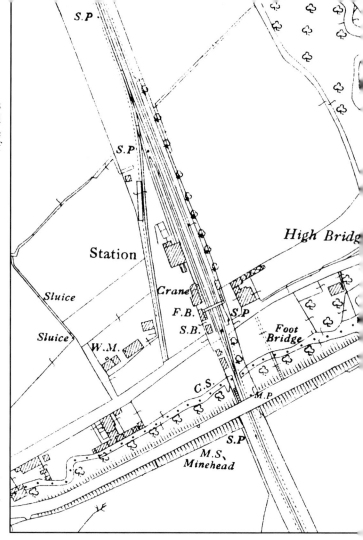

44.   No. D6336 runs in from Minehead in about 1964 and passes the redundant water column, which was soon removed. (C.L.Caddy coll.)

45.   A southward panorama on 30th October 1965 includes the other water tank, but it is largely obscured by the footbridge. The loop was shortened beyond the footbridge in 1968. (C.L.Caddy)

46.   This is the last day of BR operation, hence the photographers. The fine barge boards date from the opulent days of the Victorian era. (C.L.Caddy)

47.   In the early years of revival, some small industrial locomotives were employed. Seen on 24th April 1983 is Hudswell Clarke no. 1731 *Jennifer*, which had been built in 1942. (T.Heavyside)

48.   It is 11th September 1987 and 2-8-0 no. 53808 is working between Minehead and Williton, while the DMU is providing the connection to Bishop's Lydeard. Oak Shag would have been a mystery to many, as would an electric gas lamp. (T.Heavyside)

49.   Seen on the same day is 2-6-2T no. 5572 in splendid condition, like the station with its
hanging baskets. The young man was enjoying Gala Week, as well as the mystery of wicker baskets.
(T.Heavyside)

50.   The great length of the loop is evident as the now familiar 2-8-0 no. 5308 arrives with an immaculate GWR-style chocolate and cream train on 10th April 1988. The WSR was attracting vast crowds with such high standards. (T.Heavyside)

➔ 51. The Diesel & Electric Group established its base here and it is seen from an up train on 16th April 1990. The siding had been closed in 1965 following freight service withdrawal in July 1964. It was reinstated for engineers use in 1968-71. The footbridge from Trowbridge was re-erected here and opened on 16th July 2011. (V.Mitchell)

➔ 52. Even in the rain on 31st October 1991, one could admire the perfect presentation of the rolling stock and signalling. Few stations could offer details of distempers for decorators, as they were last used 40 years earlier. (T.Heavyside)

53.   Following closure of Swindon Works in 1986, a building from the locomotive stores was rebuilt here in 1991, for use as a maintenance depot. Shown on 20th July 1992, no. 53808 had reverted to its original livery and number, but the impressive station had changed little. (T.Heavyside)

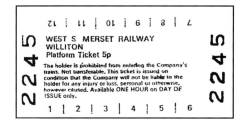

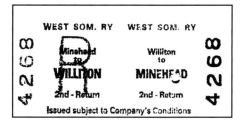

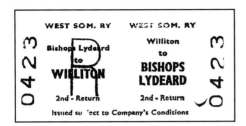

54.	A panorama from the road bridge on 9th March 1996, has the site of the level crossing in the foreground. No. 44422 is working freight on a S&DJR themed weekend. The visitor centre was created in the goods shed just beyond the main building and the WSRA workshop can be seen on the left. The box has a 25-lever frame. (T.Heavyside)

DONIFORD HALT

55.   This is a request stop, but 2-6-2T no. 4561 passes through with a demonstration freight train bound for Minehead on 23rd March 1997. The stop was opened as "Doniford Beach Halt" on 27th June 1987, but was soon closed, owing to problems with the access path. It was reopened on 14th July 1992, but devoid of the word "Beach". (T.Heavyside)

56.　　Running in the opposite direction on the same day is 2-6-0 no. 7325. Both views are from the road bridge. Beautiful panoramas abound in this area. (T.Heavyside)

57.   The halt is seen from the rear of an ex-GWR autocoach on 30th December 2006. When propelled, the driver would sit on the right, with the vacuum brake in front of him. The regulator and hand brake are near the centre window. (M.Dunse)

58.   Erected near the platform in 1990 is this fine Pagoda shelter, once common on the GWR. Approaching on 28th December 2008 is ex-GWR 2-8-0 no. 3850. 179 is the mileage from Paddington. (A.Padfield)

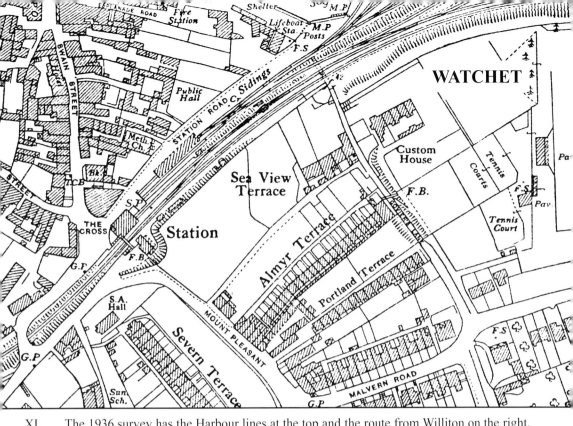

XI.   The 1936 survey has the Harbour lines at the top and the route from Williton on the right. The long shed near the word STATION of Station Road had no walls; it was a covered loading platform.

59.   The cranes indicate the position of the harbour as no. 3440 waits with the 12.20 Bishop's Lydeard to Minehead on 21st July 1992. The tall building on the left is the Methodist Church. (T.Heavyside)

60.   The end of the goods shed is again evident as we enjoy the sight of no. 3440 *City of Truro* departing west on 19th July 1992. Its speed record was 102.3mph in 1904. (T.Heavyside)

Extract from Bradshaw's Guide for 1866.
(Reprinted by Middleton Press 2011)

WATCHET.

Telegraph station at Taunton.

A coast guard station, prettily seated in a secluded creek on the Bristol Channel. *Dunster Castle* and the beautiful watering place of *Minehead*, standing on the cliffs to the south, are within a very short distance. A few miles further on the same coast, but somewhat more inland, brings the tourist to the sources of the Exe, in Exmore Forest, a wild but interesting tract, where the red deer is sometimes seen.

The *West Somerset Mineral* continues this route through WASHFORD and ROADWATER to COMBE ROW.

Leaving the Taunton station we are subjected for a short time to the confinement of a cutting, on passing which we perceive the Bridgewater and Taunton canal on our left, while the eminences to our right are crowned with picturesque villages. Proceeding on an embankment, the little hamlet of Bishop's Hall is passed, and we soon after cross several streams tributary to the Tone, that gleam and sparkle between the patches of meadow land and forest scenery by which they are skirted in their progress. After crossing a viaduct over the Tone, the arch of Shaw bridge, and passing an excavation, we are carried forward by a sinuous embankment

61.   A photograph from the footbridge two days later features the ex-S&DJR 2-8-0 no. 88 and
the bridge from which the previous two pictures were taken. (T.Heavyside)

WEST SOMERSET RAILWAY

Bishops Lydeard to
MINEHEAD

283

PONTIN'S EXPRESS

30 September 1981

Issued subject to
Company conditions   **ADULT £2·40 return**

62.   Nos 51485 and 56121 were working the 09.55 from Bishop's Lydeard on 30th April 1994. The DMU will soon pass over the trackbed of the West Somerset Mineral Railway. It closed in 1910 and is featured in *Branch Line to Minehead*. It has been converted to a splendid public footpath. (T.Heavyside)

63.   Although goods traffic ceased on 16th May 1965, the goods shed remained standing to be photographed in 2012 in use as a boat museum. (R.Williams)

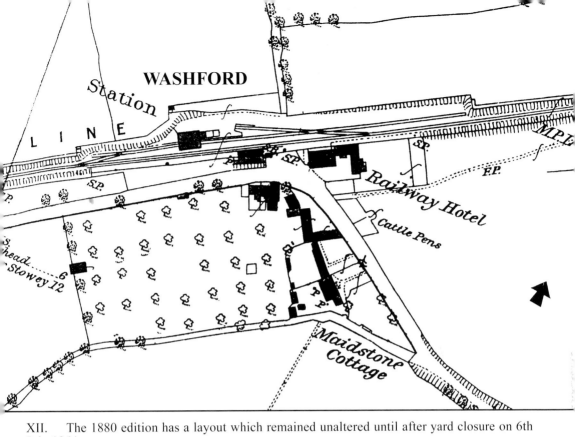

WASHFORD

XII.   The 1880 edition has a layout which remained unaltered until after yard closure on 6th July 1964.

64.   A record from 30th October 1965 features the tiny signal box, which had closed in 1952. (C.L.Caddy)

65.   A DMU bound for Minehead is seen on 2nd January 1971. Nearest is the lamp hut, where pressurised Tilley lamps were prepared for hoisting up the posts, using the winch on the post. (E. Wilmshurst)

66.   A small crowd waits on the same day for a train to Taunton. The yard would soon have a new life. The station had been unstaffed since 21st February 1966 and was thus unlit. (E. Wilmshurst)

67.   How times change! It is 20th June 1977 and the Somerset & Dorset Railway Trust had adopted the premises in 1975. Its collection was moved from Radstock and it soon established a museum in the station building. (T.Heavyside)

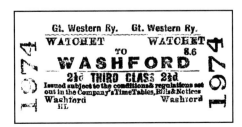

68.   The S&DRT workshop was erected over one of the new sidings and can be seen above class
5100 2-6-2T no. 4160 on 21st March 1997. This locomotive had been built by BR to a GWR design.
(T.Heavyside)

69.   A rare through train from Paddington was recorded on 23rd March 1997, running to Minehead as part of the Gala. It is now clear that the station is on the side of a valley. (T.Heavyside)

70.   We continue our visit to this very remarkable location with four views from the weekend of 18th March 2006. In steam was Hawthorn Leslie no. 3437 and nearby was Peckett no. 1788. (T.Heavyside)

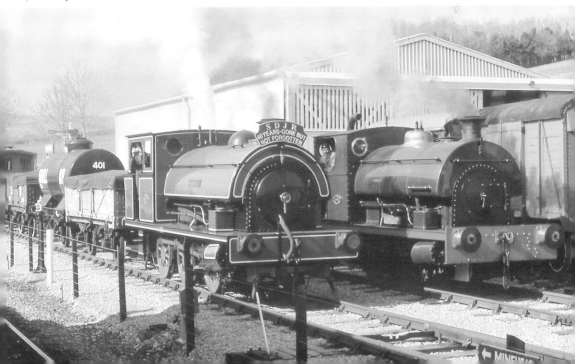

71.   The Peckett was returned to the museum shed and we can marvel at the range of ephemera on show. The locomotive had been built in 1929. (T.Heavyside)

72.   The Hawthorn Leslie carried out shunting demonstrations, the rattle of loose couplings being musical memories to many older visitors. On the left were the smaller exhibits. The small signal box had been refitted using equipment to represent Midford. (T.Heavyside)

73.   The platform had been lengthened in 1933-34, making it ideal for such remarkable photographs. Heading west are BR class 4 2-6-0 no. 76009 and "Battle of Britain" class 4-6-2 no. 34067 *Tangmere*. (T.Heavyside)

BLUE ANCHOR

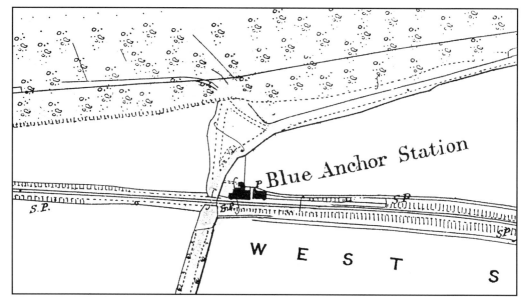

XIII.   The beach is at the top of this 1886 extract. The loop and a second platform were added in 1904. A short goods siding was completed in 1913, southwest of the level crossing.

74.   The signalman stands with the single line token as 2-8-0 no. 53808 comes to the end of the level track on 11th September 1987. The 1904 signal box and the much older station building avoided demolition. (T.Heavyside)

75.   Splendidly presented, 2-6-2T no. 5572 was in freight haulage mode on the same day. Recreational accommodation could be found both sides of the track. (T.Heavyside)

76.   No. 53808 is about to run close to the sea on its way to Minehead on 16th April 1990. The signal partially obscures Conygar Tower. The hut was for oil for the lamps on the platforms and in the signals. (V.Mitchell)

77.   Minutes later, the train departs and a volunteer carries coal for the booking office fire. Close to him are the rods which link the gate wheel in the signal box to the hidden gate links. Camping coaches stand on the left, but the relaid siding was not reconnected. (V.Mitchell)

WEST SOMERSET RAILWAY
Diesel Weekend
Saturday, 14 July 1984
THE EXMOOR ZEPHYR
Dep. Bishops Lydeard 19.15 Dep. Minehead 21.45

£................ ... .

Name ....

Coach .... Seat ....

Issued subject to Company's conditions

No.   0287   ☐O☐R☐

78.   It is no. 3440 *City of Truro* again and seldom seen in detail is the spare oil lamp which faces the smokebox base. The shelter near the milk churns was the only part which had to be rebuilt after reopening. (T.Heavyside)

79.   Nos 51880 and 51889 are in the preserved DMU livery and are approaching on 22nd April 1998. All had been perfectly restored including the Ladies, right. It was unusually distant from the booking office and was a 1904 afterthought, not unusual in those times. (T.Heavyside)

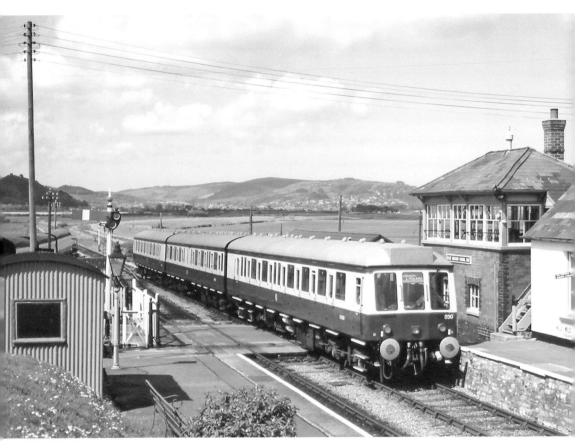

80.   The same train is seen three days later and more of the coast is visible. On the left is one of the two wicket gates which were locked shut by two levers in the signal box, just as a train approached. It meant that pedestrians would not be delayed as much as road users. (T.Heavyside)

81.   A typical milk train was on offer on 20th March 1999, hauled by 0-6-0PT no. 9466. It was the railway strike of 1955, which brought such traffic to an end. An excellent museum is in the waiting room on the left. (T.Heavyside)

82.   The entrance to the down platform is included in this view from 31st March 2001. No. 9466 is seen again as it accelerates towards Minehead. In the other direction, there is a gradient up at 1 in 541 from the station. The box has 17 levers. (T.Heavyside)

EAST OF DUNSTER

83.   With splendid views on both sides, 4-6-0 no. 6024 *King Edward I* speeds along the coastline towards Minehead on 22nd March 1997. The wind must be from the southwest. (T.Heavyside)

DUNSTER

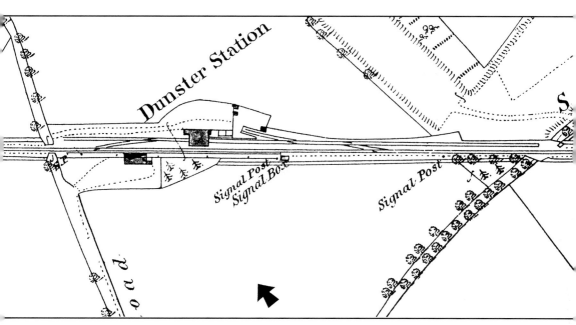

XIV.   The 1886 map has a layout which remained unchanged into the 21st century. The signal box was closed in 1926 and a new one built near the level crossing, left. There was double track from it to Minehead from 19th March 1934, but it became two single tracks from 27th March 1966. This box was retained until line closure, to control them.

84.   The GWR roof design avoided the need for canopy supports on the platform. Triangular trusses were cantilevered on the brickwork. No. 53808 had undergone much of its restoration in S&DRT workshops at Washford and is seen arriving on 10th April 1988. (T.Heavyside)

85.   Simmering gently on 31st March 2001 is ex-BR 2-6-4T no. 80136. The dock on the right once carried cattle pens; they are shown on the map. (T.Heavyside)

West Somerset Railway
CO. LTD.

18177

Minehead	Blue Anchor
to	to
Blue Anchor	Minehead
ADULT	ADULT

Is: :d subject to Company'
conditions

18177

86.   Most long distance trains did not call at the intermediate stations. Heading one on 31st March 2001 is no. 66061; it is a Hertfordshire Rail Tour from Letchworth. (T.Heavyside)

87.   Shunting for fun on 24th May 2007 is the beautiful 2-6-4T, no. 80136. It is surrounded by the WSR's sleeper stock. Prior to closure, there had been an oil storage depot beyond the goods shed. The WSR added an extra siding beyond the crossing, on the north side. (T.Heavyside)

EAST OF MINEHEAD

88.   Sea defence work demanded the conveyance of a vast tonnage of rocks from the limestone quarries at Merehead, near Frome. One load is arriving behind no. 37800 on 24th April 1998. (T.Heavyside)

89.   The same signal appears again as class B1 4-6-0 no. 61264 leaves Minehead on 31st March 2001. This type was built between 1942 and 1952. The line was double west of Dunster from 1934 to 1966. (T.Heavyside)

90.   The relief road for Minehead came into use in 1992. Called Seaward Way, it required a level crossing and automatic barriers were employed. Class 5100 2-6-2T no. 4160 is passing over it on 23rd March 2002. (T.Heavyside)

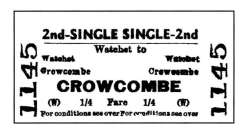

91.   The buildings are finished and 4-6-0 no. 7822 *Foxcote Manor* runs in reverse on 24th March 2007. The triangle seen earlier and the turntable would soon eliminate such discomfort to enginemen. (T.Heavyside)

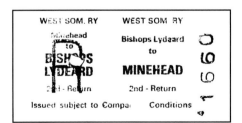

→ 92. Class 03 no. D2133 was Minehead pilot engine on 13th April 2011 and it is seen on the cattle grid of the new crosssing, a feature seldom recorded. (C.Harris)

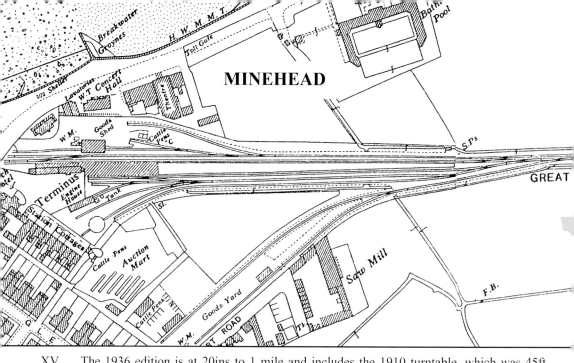

MINEHEAD

GREAT

XV.   The 1936 edition is at 20ins to 1 mile and includes the 1910 turntable, which was 45ft in length. It was in place until 1966. The engine "house" was in use until 1956 and C marks the position of the 6-ton crane.

93.   The 10.50 departure to Taunton was recorded on 5th September 1960, with 4500 class 2-6-2T no. 5548 in attendance. Goods traffic ceased on 6th July 1964. (T.Heavyside)

94.　　After extension in 1934, the main platform could accommodate 16 coaches. Class 5100 2-6-2T no. 4143 is waiting with coaches destined for Taunton and Paddington in August 1963. (R.E.Toop)

95.　　This is the view from the buffer stops on 30th October 1965. At least there were many mailbags to be loaded. The building had been tastefully extended towards us in the 1930s. (C.L.Caddy)

96.   The desolate site is seen in the early 1970s. The higher canopy served both platforms. Both run-round loops were retained, but the line nearest to us was shortened. The two single lines were controlled from Dunster. (N.Jones)

➔   97. This is our first view after takeover by the WSR. The platform lines and loops remained, but all the sidings had to be relaid. Departing on 20th June 1977 is 0-6-0PT no. 6412 and sheeted up on the left is no. 53808. (T.Heavyside)

➔   98. The 1934 signal box had been on the north side of the line here, but was demolished after the two single lines were created in 1966. The enterprising WSR needed one here and so it moved the Dunster box here on 20th November 1977. It is seen on 28th May 1978. Prior to going to Dunster in 1934, it had served in South Wales. (J.Cornelius)

WEST SOMERSET RAILWAY

FIFTY PENCE

SINGLE

Issued subject to Company's Conditions

99.   The shorter platform was known as The Bay and numbered 2. We look at it from near the buffers in about 1982, as the Cravens 2-car DMU waits for visitors to enjoy the journey. (R.Hicks)

→   100.   The joy of the S&DRT is seen on 11th September 1987, after its eight-year restoration at Washford. It is outside the former goods shed. The old engine shed had long gone. Minehead is home to Butlins Holiday Camp. It accommodated 4-6-0 no. 6229 *Duchess of Hamilton* and 0-6-2T no. 78 *Knowle* of the "Terrier" class until 1975. They are now preserved elsewhere. (T.Heavyside)

→   101.   Standing at platform 1 on 13th September 1987 is Bagnall 0-6-0ST no. 2996 *Victor*. It is piloting class 4500 no. 5572 on the 125th anniversary year of the Watchet to Taunton section. A traditional booking hall interior came from Cardiff Central that year. (T.Heavyside)

WEST SOMERSET RAILWAY
Minehead
to
TAUNTON
2nd - Single   2nd - Single
Issued subject to Company's Conditions

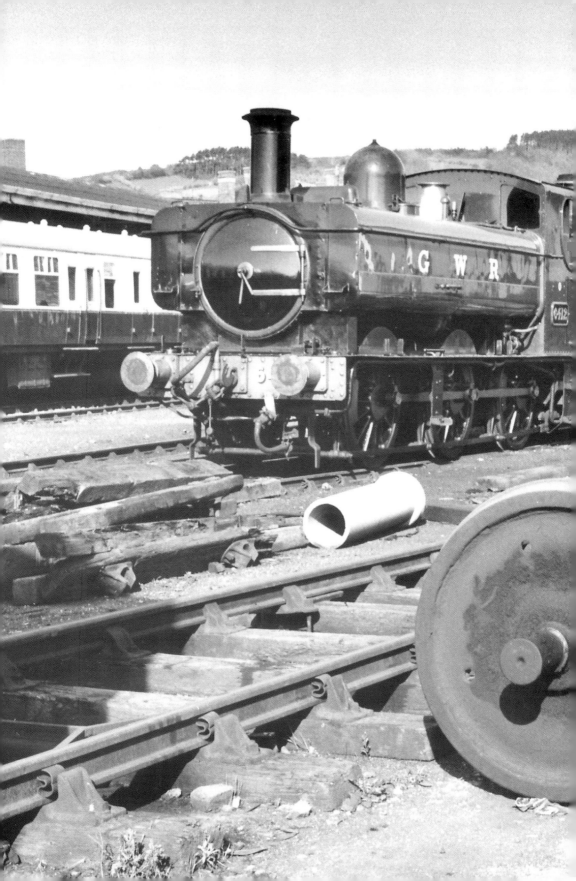

102.   It is 10th April 1988 and outside the engine shed is 0-6-0 no. 3205, while in front of it is 0-6-0PT no. 6412. The depot undertakes most maintenance work, with the exception of major boiler repairs. (T.Heavyside)

103.   The extent of the depot becomes apparent as we move down the platform, before the departing DMU obstructs the view. The cattle pens and the crane had been on the right. The date is 10th April 1988. (T.Heavyside)

104.   Seldom is a bygone age captured so dramatically without supplementary lighting. The Cravens DMU is at rest in the bay platform on the evening of 31st October 1992. (S.Edge)

105.   Giving the impression of a main line depot, the yard was busy on 23rd March 1997. Present were nos 7820, 7760, 7325, and 3205. A second water tank is available in the distance. (T.Heavyside)

106.   The bay is holding a particularly long train on 19th March 1999. At its head is 0-6-0PT no. 6412. (T.Heavyside)

107.   The 1998 extension to the engine shed is seen on 20th March 2005. From left to right we have 0-6-0PT no. 6412 and 2-6-2Ts nos 5553 and 5542. (T.Heavyside)

108.   Crowds abound on 24th March 2007 and nos 5553 and 5521 bark for their pleasure. The need for more carriage accommodation is evident. The box was refitted to working order in 1990. (T.Heavyside)

109.   The former Pwllheli turntable had been purchased and it can be seen in picture 105 in the *Barmouth to Pwllheli* Middleton Press album. It had been stored near the signal box and is seen in transit to the locomotive yard on 9th July 2007. No. D2133 is hauling it, prior to its despatch by road for rebuilding. (M. Snell)

110.   An unusual delivery took place on 10th February 2008, when the Pwllheli turntable arrived back. It is seen at Cross Keys, on the A358 northwest of Taunton. (M.Anderson)

111.   During its retirement, the turntable was extended to 65ft. Its width remained suitable for A roads, under police supervision. It is about to pass over Doniford Stream on the same day and is seen from the WSR bridge, one mile south of Williton station. (M.Southwood)

112.   The most dramatic day in the turntable story was 11th February 2008. Words are not needed. (M.Stacey)

1977

TABLE 3			Ⓢ	TWFO Watchet Explorer		Ⓢ	Ⓢ		MThO
MINEHEAD dep.	09.15	**10.35**	11.25	12.30	**14.35**	**15.40**	16.30	17.45
Dunster dep.	09.20	**10.41**	11.30	12.35	**14.41**	**15.46**	16.35	17.50
Blue Anchor arr.	09.26	**10.48**	11.36	12.41	**14.48**	**15.53**	16.41	17.56
dep.	09.27		11.37	12.42			16.42	17.57
Washford dep.	09.34		11.44	12.49			16.49	18.04
Watchet dep.	09.41		11a51	12.56			16.56	18a10
Williton arr.	09.46		—	13.01			17.01	—

				TWFO					MThO
Williton dep.	09.55		—	13.55			17.05	
Watchet dep.	10.01		11.55	14.01			17.11	18.15
Washford dep.	10.08		12.02	14.08			17.18	18.22
Blue Anchor arr.	10.14	Ⓢ	12.08	14.14	Ⓢ	Ⓢ	17.24	18.28
dep.	10.15	**11.05**	12.10	14.15	**15.05**	**16.10**	17.25	18.29
Dunster dep.	10.21	**11.13**	12.16	14.21	**15.13**	**16.18**	17.31	18.35
MINEHEAD arr.	10.27	**11.19**	12.22	14.27	**15.19**	**16.24**	17.37	18.40

Mondays to Fridays 8 June—22 July

TWFO—Tuesdays, Wednesdays, Fridays only   MThO—Mondays, Thursdays only

Steam hauled trains are identified by the symbol Ⓢ

113.   The turntable was passed for use on 11th December 2008 and is seen in May 2009, with a roundabout sign to add humour. The deviation in the platform edge is intentional; it accommodates the massive cylinders of ex-GWR engines when on the curve of the points. (A.Dorrington)

114.   The admirable restoration of the signal box is visible only to the selected few and so it appears here. The frame has 27 levers. (D.Oldham)

115.   Ex-GWR 4-6-0 no. 6024 *King Edward I* heads for the turntable as class 52 no. D1015 *Western Champion* prepares to shunt the London train stock on 19th June 2010. No wonder that the WSR can attract the crowds! A water tank was completed near the turntable in 2012. This meant that engines needing water did not have to cross the running lines or obstruct Seaward Way crossing. (Sylvia Way)

➔   116. No. 59206 has just run round its stone train on 8th December 2010 and is leaving prior to it being unloaded down the line. This took 2½ to 3 hours. The view is from the signal box. (M.Southwood)

➔   117. This is the oldest part of the building and is at the east end. The doors gave access to the booking hall in BR days, but visitors were welcomed at the west end when the photograph was taken in 2008. (P.Nicholson)

118.   A Southern Railway scene was created at Minehead on 3rd May 2011, with SR 4-6-2 no. 34046 *Braunton* on the turntable and SR 4-6-0 no. 30777 *Sir Lamiel* in the bay platform after arriving from Bishop's Lydeard with the Duke of Gloucester on board. (C.Austin)

→   119.   The length of Minehead platform is illustrated by the fact that class 47 no. D1661 heads the seven coach 5.35pm from Minehead (reversed back to the buffer stops), but is still dwarfed by the platform. Seen here on the 4th August 2012 is the 1991 carriage shed, on the right. (R.White)

→   120. A view from Seaward Way level crossing towards a snow covered Minehead Station on 18th December 2010, features a peaceful scene that has given so much pleasure to countless people. Long may it continue and congratulations to all those involved. (K.Sanders)

Other views of these stations can be enjoyed in the Middleton Press album *Branch Line to Minehead,* **which includes many earlier photographs.**

MP MIDDLETON Press

EVOLVING THE ULTIMATE RAIL ENCYCLOPEDIA

Easebourne Lane, Midhurst, West Sussex.
GU29 9AZ   Tel:01730 813169
www.middletonpress.co.uk   email:info@middletonpress.co.uk
A-978 0 906520 B- 978 1 873793 C- 978 1 901706 D-978 1 904474
E - 978 1 906008   F - 978 1 908174

All titles listed below were in print at time of publication - please check current availability by looking at our website - www.middletonpress.co.uk or by requesting a Brochure which includes our LATEST RAILWAY TITLES also our TRAMWAY, TROLLEYBUS, MILITARY and COASTAL series

A
Abergavenny to Merthyr C 91 8
Abertillery & Ebbw Vale Lines D 84 5
Aberystwyth to Carmarthen E 90 1
Allhallows - Branch Line to A 62 8
Alton - Branch Lines to A 11 6
Andover to Southampton A 82 6
Ascot - Branch Lines around A 64 2
Ashburton - Branch Line to B 95 4
Ashford - Steam to Eurostar B 67 1
Ashford to Dover A 48 2
Austrian Narrow Gauge D 04 3
Avonmouth - BL around D 42 5
Aylesbury to Rugby D 91 3

B
Baker Street to Uxbridge D 90 6
Bala to Llandudno E 87 1
Banbury to Birmingham D 27 2
Banbury to Cheltenham E 63 5
Bangor to Holyhead F 01 7
Bangor to Portmadoc E 72 7
Barking to Southend C 80 2
Barmouth to Pwllheli E 53 6
Barry - Branch Lines around D 50 0
Bartlow - Branch Lines to F 27 7
Bath Green Park to Bristol C 36 9
Bath to Evercreech Junction A 60 4
Beamish 40 years on rails E94 9
Bedford to Wellingborough D 31 9
Birmingham to Wolverhampton E253
Bletchley to Cambridge D 94 4
Bletchley to Rugby E 07 9
Bodmin - Branch Lines around B 83 1
Bournemouth to Evercreech Jn A 46 8
Bournemouth to Weymouth A 57 4
Bradshaw's Guide 1866 F 05 5
Bradshaw's History F18 5
Bradshaw's Rail Times 1850 F 13 0
Bradshaw's Rail Times 1895 F 11 6
Branch Lines series - see town names
Brecon to Neath D 43 2
Brecon to Newport D 16 6
Brecon to Newtown E 06 2
Brighton to Eastbourne A 16 1
Brighton to Worthing A 03 1
Bristol to Taunton D 03 6
Bromley South to Rochester B 23 7
Bromsgrove to Birmingham D 87 6
Bromsgrove to Gloucester D 73 9
Broxbourne to Cambridge F16 1
Brunel - a railtour D 74 6
Bude - Branch Line to B 29 9
Burnham to Evercreech Jn B 68 0

C
Cambridge to Ely D 55 5
Canterbury - BLs around B 58 9
Cardiff to Dowlais (Cae Harris) E 47 5
Cardiff to Pontypridd E 95 6
Cardiff to Swansea E 42 0
Carlisle to Hawick E 85 7
Carmarthen to Fishguard E 66 6
Caterham & Tattenham Corner B251
Central & Southern Spain NG E 91 8
Chard and Yeovil - BLs a C 30 7
Charing Cross to Dartford A 75 8
Charing Cross to Orpington A 96 3
Cheddar - Branch Line to B 90 9
Cheltenham to Andover C 43 7
Cheltenham to Redditch D 81 4
Chester to Birkenhead F 21 5
Chester to Rhyl E 93 2
Chichester to Portsmouth A 14 7
Clacton and Walton - BLs to F 04 8

Clapham Jn to Beckenham Jn B 36 7
Cleobury Mortimer - BLs a E 18 5
Clevedon & Portishead - BLs to D180
Consett to South Shields E 57 4
Cornwall Narrow Gauge D 56 2
Corris and Vale of Rheidol E 65 9
Craven Arms to Llandeilo E 35 2
Craven Arms to Wellington E 33 8
Crawley to Littlehampton A 34 5
Cromer - Branch Lines around C 26 0
Croydon to East Grinstead B 48 0
Crystal Palace & Catford Loop B 87 1
Cyprus Narrow Gauge E 13 0

D
Darjeeling Revisited F 09 3
Darlington Leamside Newcastle E 28 4
Darlington to Newcastle D 98 2
Dartford to Sittingbourne B 34 3
Denbigh - Branch Lines around F 32 1
Derwent Valley - BL to the D 06 7
Devon Narrow Gauge E 09 3
Didcot to Banbury D 02 9
Didcot to Swindon C 84 0
Didcot to Winchester C 13 0
Dorset & Somerset NG D 76 0
Douglas - Laxey - Ramsey E 75 8
Douglas to Peel C 88 8
Douglas to Port Erin C 55 0
Douglas to Ramsey D 39 5
Dover to Ramsgate A 78 9
Dublin Northwards in 1950s E 31 4
Dunstable - Branch Lines to E 27 7

E
Ealing to Slough C 42 0
Eastbourne to Hastings A 27 7
East Cornwall Mineral Railways D 22 7
East Croydon to Three Bridges A 53 6
Eastern Spain Narrow Gauge E 56 7
East Grinstead - BLs to A 07 9
East London - Branch Lines of C 44 4
East London Line B 80 0
East of Norwich - Branch Lines E 69 7
Effingham Junction - BLs a A 74 1
Ely to Norwich C 90 1
Enfield Town & Palace Gates D 32 6
Epsom to Horsham A 30 7
Eritrean Narrow Gauge E 38 3
Euston to Harrow & Wealdstone C 89 5
Exeter to Barnstaple B 15 2
Exeter to Newton Abbot C 49 9
Exeter to Tavistock B 69 5
Exmouth - Branch Lines to B 00 8

F
Fairford - Branch Line to A 52 9
Falmouth, Helston & St. Ives C 74 1
Fareham to Salisbury A 67 3
Faversham to Dover B 05 3
Felixstowe & Aldeburgh - BL to D 20 3
Fenchurch Street to Barking C 20 8
Festiniog - 50 yrs of enterprise C 83 3
Festiniog 1946-55 E 01 7
Festiniog in the Fifties B 68 8
Festiniog in the Sixties B 91 6
Ffestiniog in Colour 1955-82 F 25 3
Finsbury Park to Alexandra Pal C 02 8
Frome to Bristol B 77 0

G
Gloucester to Bristol D 35 7
Gloucester to Cardiff D 66 1
Gosport - Branch Lines around A 36 9
Greece Narrow Gauge D 72 2

H

Hampshire Narrow Gauge D 36 4
Harrow to Watford D 14 2
Harwich & Hadleigh - BLs to F 02 4
Hastings to Ashford A 37 6
Hawick to Galashiels F 36 9
Hawkhurst - Branch Line to A 66 6
Hayling - Branch Line to A 12 3
Hay-on-Wye - BL around D 92 0
Haywards Heath to Seaford A 28 4
Hemel Hempstead - BLs to D 88 3
Henley, Windsor & Marlow - BLa C77 2
Hereford to Newport D 54 8
Hertford & Hatfield - BLs a E 58 1
Hertford Loop E 71 0
Hexham to Carlisle D 75 3
Hexham to Hawick F 08 6
Hitchin to Peterborough D 07 4
Holborn Viaduct to Lewisham A 81 9
Horsham - Branch Lines to A 02 4
Huntingdon - Branch Line to A 93 2

I
Ilford to Shenfield C 97 0
Ilfracombe - Branch Line to B 21 3
Industrial Rlys of the South East A 09 3
Ipswich to Saxmundham C 41 3
Isle of Wight Lines - 50 yrs C 12 3
Italy Narrow Gauge F 17 8

K
Kent Narrow Gauge C 45 1
Kidderminster to Shrewsbury E 10 9
Kingsbridge - Branch Line to C 98 7
Kings Cross to Potters Bar E 62 8
Kingston & Hounslow Loops A 83 3
Kingswear - Branch Line to C 17 8

L
Lambourn - Branch Line to C 70 3
Launceston & Princetown - BLs C 19 2
Lewisham to Dartford A 92 5
Lines around Wimbledon B 75 6
Liverpool Street to Chingford D 01 2
Liverpool Street to Ilford C 34 5
Llandeilo to Swansea E 46 8
London Bridge to Addiscombe B 20 6
London Bridge to East Croydon A 58 1
Longmoor - Branch Lines to A 41 3
Looe - Branch Line to C 22 2
Lowestoft - BLs around E 40 6
Ludlow to Hereford E 14 7
Lydney - Branch Lines around E 26 0
Lyme Regis - Branch Line to A 45 1
Lynton - Branch Line to B 04 6

M
Machynlleth to Barmouth E 54 3
Maesteg and Tondu Lines E 06 2
March - Branch Lines around B 09 1
Marylebone to Rickmansworth D 49 4
Melton Constable to Yarmouth Bch E031
Midhurst - Branch Lines of E 78 9
Midhurst - Branch Lines to F 00 0
Minehead - Branch Line to A 80 2
Mitcham Junction Lines B 01 5
Mitchell & company C 59 8
Monmouth - Branch Lines to E 20 8
Monmouthshire Eastern Valleys D 71 5
Moretonhampstead - BL to C 27 7
Moreton-in-Marsh to Worcester D 26 5
Mountain Ash to Neath D 80 7

N
Newbury to Westbury C 66 6
Newcastle to Hexham D 69 2
Newport (IOW) - Branch Lines to A 26 0
Newquay - Branch Lines to C 71 0
Newton Abbot to Plymouth C 60 4

Newtown to Aberystwyth E 41 3
North East German NG D 44 9
Northern Alpine Narrow Gauge F 37 6
Northern France Narrow Gauge C 75 8
Northern Spain Narrow Gauge E 83 3
North London Line B 94 7
North Woolwich - BLs around C 65 9

O
Ongar - Branch Line to E 05 5
Oswestry - Branch Lines around E 60 4
Oswestry to Whitchurch E 81 9
Oxford to Bletchley D 57 9
Oxford to Moreton-in-Marsh D 15 9

P
Paddington to Ealing C 37 6
Paddington to Princes Risborough C819
Padstow - Branch Line to B 54 1
Pembroke and Cardigan - BLs to F 29 1
Peterborough to Kings Lynn E 32 1
Plymouth - BLs around B 98 5
Plymouth to St. Austell C 63 5
Pontypool to Mountain Ash D 65 4
Pontypridd to Merthyr F 14 7
Pontypridd to Port Talbot E 86 4
Porthmadog 1954-94 - BLa B 31 2
Portmadoc 1923-46 - BLa B 13 8
Portsmouth to Southampton A 31 4
Portugal Narrow Gauge E 67 3
Potters Bar to Cambridge D 70 8
Princes Risborough - BL to D 05 0
Princes Risborough to Banbury C 85 7

R
Reading to Basingstoke B 27 5
Reading to Didcot C 79 6
Reading to Guildford A 47 5
Redhill to Ashford A 73 4
Return to Blaenau 1970-82 C 64 2
Rhyl to Bangor F 15 4
Rhymney & New Tredegar Lines E 48 2
Rickmansworth to Aylesbury D 61 6
Romania & Bulgaria NG E 23 9
Romneyrail C 32 1
Ross-on-Wye - BLs around E 30 7
Ruabon to Barmouth E 84 0
Rugby to Birmingham E 37 6
Rugby to Loughborough F 12 3
Rugby to Stafford F 07 9
Ryde to Ventnor A 19 2

S
Salisbury to Westbury B 39 8
Saxmundham to Yarmouth C 69 7
Saxony Narrow Gauge D 47 0
Seaton & Sidmouth - BLs to A 95 6
Selsey - Branch Line to A 04 8
Sheerness - Branch Line to B 16 2
Shenfield to Ipswich E 96 3
Shrewsbury - Branch Line to A 86 4
Shrewsbury to Chester E 70 3
Shrewsbury to Ludlow E 21 5
Shrewsbury to Newtown E 29 1
Sierra Leone Narrow Gauge D 28 9
Sirhowy Valley Line E 12 3
Sittingbourne to Ramsgate A 90 1
Slough to Newbury C 56 7
South African Two-foot gauge E 51 2
Southampton to Bournemouth A 42 0
Southend & Southminster BLs E 76 5
Southern Alpine Narrow Gauge F 22 2
Southern France Narrow Gauge C 47 5
South London Line B 46 6
South Lynn to Norwich City F 03 1
Southwold - Branch Line to A 15 4
Spalding - Branch Lines around E 52 9

Stafford to Chester F 34 5
St Albans to Bedford D 08 1
St. Austell to Penzance C 67 3
ST Isle of Wight A 56 7
Stourbridge to Wolverhampton
St. Pancras to Barking D 68 5
St. Pancras to Folkestone E 88
St. Pancras to St. Albans C 78
Stratford-u-Avon to Birmingha
Stratford-u-Avon to Cheltenhar
ST West Hants A 69 7
Sudbury - Branch Lines to F 1
Surrey Narrow Gauge C 87 1
Sussex Narrow Gauge C 68 0
Swanley to Ashford B 45 9
Swansea - Branch Lines around
Swansea to Carmarthen E 59
Swindon to Bristol C 96 3
Swindon to Gloucester D 46 3
Swindon to Newport D 30 2
Swiss Narrow Gauge C 94 9

T
Talyllyn 60 E 98 7
Taunton to Barnstaple B 60 2
Taunton to Exeter C 82 6
Taunton to Minehead F 39 0
Tavistock to Plymouth B 88 6
Tenterden - Branch Line to a 2
Three Bridges to Brighton A 35
Tilbury Loop C 86 4
Tiverton - BLs around C 62 8
Tivetshall to Beccles D 41 8
Tonbridge to Hastings A 44 4
Torrington - Branch Lines to B
Towcester - BLs around E 39 (
Tunbridge Wells BLs A 32 1

U
Upwell - Branch Line to B 64 (

V
Victoria to Bromley South A 98
Vivarais Revisited E 08 6

W
Wantage - Branch Line to D 25
Wareham to Swanage 50 yrs
Waterloo to Windsor A 54 3
Waterloo to Woking A 38 3
Watford to Leighton Buzzard D
Welshpool to Llanfair E 49 9
Wenford Bridge to Fowey C 09
Westbury to Bath B 55 8
Westbury to Taunton C 76 5
West Cornwall Mineral Rlys D
West Croydon to Epsom B 08
West German Narrow Gauge D
West London - BLs of C 50 5
West London Line B 84 8
West London Line B 848
West Wiltshire - BLs of D 12 8
Weymouth - BLs A 65 9
Willesden Jn to Richmond B 7
Wimbledon to Beckenham C 5
Wimbledon to Epsom B 62 6
Wimborne - BLs around A 97
Wisbech - BLs around C 01 7
Witham & Kelvedon - BLs a E
Woking to Alton A 59 8
Woking to Portsmouth A 25 3
Woking to Southampton A 55
Wolverhampton to Shrewsbury
Worcester to Birmingham D 9
Worcester to Hereford D 38 8
Worthing to Chichester A 06 2
Wroxham - BLs around F 31 4

Y
Yeovil - 50 yrs change C 38 3
Yeovil to Dorchester A 76 5
Yeovil to Exeter A 91 8
York to Scarborough F 23 9